Endorsements

Pastor Ejaz Nabie, a biblical scholar of international repute, draws on decades of profound knowledge and experience to present *The Overflow Life* as a compelling blueprint for spiritual living. With great diligence and insight, he explores the multifaceted biblical dimensions of overflow, showing readers how to remain faithful, fruitful, and spiritually grounded through life's daily trials and discouragements. This powerful book reveals that a strong, sincere relationship with God is the key to experiencing His unlimited, never-ending, abundant overflow. *The Overflow Life* is an indispensable must-read for anyone seeking to please the Lord, rise above life's challenges, and live as a true vessel and role model for His glory.

—**Dr. Taj Rajkumar**, Retired Associate Dean of Students and Professor

Rooted in a lifetime of faithful ministry, *The Overflow Life,* by my friend and fellow pastor, Ejaz Nabie, powerfully reminds us that we are the vessel while God is the Source, and what fills us will inevitably overflow into every part of our lives. With clarity and spiritual depth, Ejaz invites you to move beyond fleeting happiness into a deep, abiding joy found in Christ, making it a must-read for anyone longing for deeper spiritual formation.

—**Wade Mumm, PhD**, Vice President, Assemblies of God Theological Seminary & Senior Pastor Greenway Church, Kissimmee FL

Simply saying "inspiring" is not sufficient to describe the power of this book. It's biblically based, soul searching, and confrontationally restorative. The word pictures are impacting. It surely changed something in me, lifting me up so I want to overflow with the love and power of Jesus Christ. I am proud to be a friend of Pastor Ejaz. Every reader will be impacted by these truths.

—**Rev. Haniff Bacchus**, Pastor, Calvary Assembly of God, Ozone Park, NY

The Overflow Life is "simplistic brilliance" that embodies the wisdom of a life well-lived in the transformative presence of God. It is a beautiful invitation to embark upon a life-altering, "journey back to the heart of Jesus." This book is a must-read for all longing for a refreshing reset to a life filled with overflowing joy.

—**Rev. Gabrielle Beam**, Founder, The Rivers Church, Saturate Bridgeport, & Rise To Read Inc.

In his book, *The Overflow Life*, Pastor Ejaz Nabie dives deep and captures the principle of overflow as taught by Jesus. The application of these life lessons empowers the believer to live faithfully, fruitfully, and fervently, as we approach the finish line. This is truly a blessing to every citizen of the Kingdom.

—**Rev. Andrew Jagessar**, Pastor, The Worship Center of Queens, Richmond Hill, NY

The overflow life indeed brings joy unspeakable, unshakable and unchangeable, and full of glory. This book produces the possibility of the overflow life, points to the place of the overflow, ignites a passion for the overflow, encourages the purity required for the overflow, leads us to the place of the overflow, but most of all, connects us with the Person (Source) of the overflow. This is not just a must-read book, but a must-lived life that impacts our families, communities, churches, and nations. Timely word-based and word-laced nuggets given to the body of Christ by the Holy Spirit through his servant Ejaz Nabie.

—**Rev. Selwyn Sills**, Pastor, Praise Tabernacle,
Linden, Guyana

The Overflow Life is an inspiring and uplifting guide that calls us to embrace a life of true abundance rooted in faith, purpose, and gratitude for God's Word and the precious presence of the Holy Spirit. Having known Pastor Ejaz Nabie for many years, I can personally affirm the depth and authenticity of his message. He offers profound yet practical insights that equip believers to walk in the fullness of the Holy Spirit and to discover and live out their God-given potential each day in Christ.

—**Rev. A. Samad Ali**, Lead Pastor,
Calvary Kissimmee Church, FL

As the Founder of the Historical Bible Society, I have had the blessing of sharing the pulpit at Faith Assembly. Pastor Ejaz Nabie and his wonderful team demonstrated a profound commitment to preaching the Gospel in a multicultural society, willing to stand up for the truth and historicity of the Gospel. Beginning his life deeply rooted in the Muslim community, this man has shown exceptional courage in taking a stand for an accurate understanding of Jesus Christ. This book expounds upon the supreme importance of staying connected to "The Vine," Jesus Christ (John 15), through the life-sustaining "sap" of the Holy Spirit. It serves as a practical "road map" for successful Christian living, with the promise an abundance of spiritual fruit (Galatians 5:22) which Christ expects all of His children to produce. This is recommended reading for anyone seeking to understand the role of the Holy Spirit in the life of the believer.

—**Daniel P. Buttafuoco**, JD, BA, MPS

THE OVERFLOW *Life*

How God Heals, Fills, and Uses Your Life
to Release Joy to the World

EJAZ NABIE
FOREWORD BY DR. MAC PIER

Orlando, Florida

Printed in the United States of America

ISBN: 979-8-9855197-7-8

Billion Soul Publishing
Orlando, Florida
www.billionsoulpub.com

Dedication

To my sons, Arik and Kevin, and my daughter-in-law, Samantha:

You are my strength, my comfort, and one of God's greatest blessings in my life. Through seasons of joy and moments of hardship, your love, encouragement, and unwavering support have been a steady refuge for me. Each of you reflects the grace and faithfulness of God in such a beautiful way, and I am deeply grateful for the bond we share as family.

This work is dedicated to you with all my love and heartfelt gratitude.

Dedication

Table of Contents

Foreword

Pastor Ejaz Nabie is one of my favorite colleagues anywhere in the world. We both live in Queens, New York City. We both live in profoundly diverse international communities. We have both served our city for four decades and travelled the globe.

It has been said that what makes a great sermon is a great life. This book, *The Overflow Life*, is a great book because Ejaz has lived a great life.

Ejaz has a profound appreciation for the Gospel, coming from a Muslim background. He knows what it means to experience the rejection of family in order to follow Jesus. Carrying one's cross is not an abstraction for Ejaz. He has joyfully carried his cross for the One who joyfully carried His cross.

The Overflow Life is the fruit of a well-lived journey. Dr. Tim Keller famously said in his book, *Center Church*, that God's goal for us is not primarily faithfulness but fruitfulness. This book is a pathway to a more fruitful life.

Fruitfulness is rooted in going deeper with God. The width of our influence for God is proportionate to the depth of our intimacy with God.

This book is an invitation to going deeper through introspection about the state of our soul. We are invited to examine the "cracks" in our soul from disappointments, hurts, and tragedies. We are invited to lean into the sufficiency of Jesus.

This book is also about going wider through service and mission. We are given a guide to follow better and to lead better. The world is desperate for lives that overflow with the fragrance of Jesus.

If you desire to live consequentially, I urge you to read this book. If you desire to make the greatest impact with the one life you've been given, apply the principles of this book.

Taking the time to read Ejaz's reflections may be the best usage of your time this year.

—**Dr. Mac Pier**, Founder, Movement.org

INTRODUCTION

Filled by God – Flowing to Others

Have you ever felt like you were giving more than you had? Like you were pouring out encouragement, love, leadership, parenting, ministry, or service … yet inside you were tired, stretched, or even empty?

Most believers know what it feels like to run on fumes. To feel the pressure to be strong while quietly feeling drained. To appear full while privately leaking.

And yet, Jesus makes us a startling promise:

> **"I have told you these things so that you will be filled with my joy. Yes, your joy will overflow!" (John 15:11, NLT).**

Overflow.
Not survival.
Not barely enough.
Not almost empty.
Overflow.

> **"I have been crucified with Christ and I no longer live, but Christ lives in me" (Galatians 2:20).**

> **"So then, just as you received Christ Jesus as Lord, continue to live your lives in him, rooted and built up in him" (Colossians 2:6–7).**

The Christian life is not merely imitation of Christ—it is participation in Christ. Through faith and the work of the Holy Spirit, believers are united with Jesus Himself. His life becomes our life. His righteousness becomes our righteousness. His joy becomes our joy. Overflow begins when we realize that the Christian life is not sustained by human strength but by divine life flowing through us.

Jesus did not call us to an exhausted life, but an **abundant** one. He did not design us to scrape by spiritually, but to **spill over** with His life, His peace, His presence, and His joy.

Overflow is not a distant dream. It is a Kingdom reality—promised, modeled, and made available by Christ Himself. But overflow does not happen by accident.

Every overflow requires a **container**.

YOUR LIFE IS A CONTAINER

Imagine your life as a vessel—a container God longs to fill. Scripture uses this imagery again and again:

- "We have this treasure in earthen vessels" (2 Corinthians 4:7).
- "Be vessels for honorable use" (2 Timothy 2:21).
- "My cup overflows" (Psalm 23:5).
- "Out of your belly will flow rivers of living water" (John 7:38).

Your life is a container shaped to carry God's presence. But like any container, it can be:

- strong or cracked
- clean or contaminated
- open or blocked
- full or empty
- overflowing or slowly leaking

God does not pour overflow into broken, neglected, or leaking vessels—not because He is unwilling but because the vessel cannot hold it.

Before God fills, He forms.
Before He pours, He repairs.
Before He overflows, He strengthens.

EVERY CONTAINER HAS LEAKS

Many believers love God sincerely, pray consistently, and serve faithfully … yet they still feel empty. Why?

Because there are leaks.

Leaks like:

- wounds never healed
- sin never confessed
- habits never disciplined
- emotions never processed
- boundaries never strengthened
- spiritual practices never cultivated

These leaks drain joy, peace, and strength faster than we can fill them. They prevent the very overflow Jesus promised.

This book will help you **identify and repair the leaks** that keep you from living full.

OVERFLOW REQUIRES POURING—DAILY, CONSISTENTLY, INTENTIONALLY

No container fills itself.
No life grows by accident.
No joy appears without cultivation.

What you pour into your heart determines what flows out of your life.

If you pour in:

- the Word of God
- the presence of God
- the love of God
- healthy relationships
- wise rhythms
- truth, not lies
- rest, not exhaustion
- purpose, not drifting

… you will fill.

If you pour long enough, consistently enough, and faithfully enough—**you will overflow.** This book will show you how.

OVERFLOW IS NOT ABOUT HAVING MORE—IT'S ABOUT BECOMING MORE

Some read "overflow" and imagine money, promotion, influence, or success. But biblical overflow is deeper, richer, and far more transformative.

Overflow is when the life of Christ inside you becomes so abundant it spills over to everyone around you.

It is:

- joy you cannot contain
- peace that steadies others
- wisdom that blesses
- love that heals
- generosity that transforms
- presence that shifts atmospheres

People with overflow bring life wherever they go. They carry the fragrance of Christ.
They serve without burning out.
They lead without being drained.
They give without anxiety.
They love without fear.

Overflowing believers are rivers, not reservoirs; conduits, not containers.

ILLUSTRATION —THE EMPTY WELL

A village once depended on a single well for water. During a drought, people kept drawing water until the well was nearly dry. One elderly man stopped them and said, "You are drawing faster than the spring can refill."

The problem was not the well—it was the pace of withdrawal without replenishment. Many believers live this way spiritually.

OVERFLOW TOUCHES THE WORLD

A life that overflows with God's presence becomes:

- a refuge for the hurting
- a light for the dark

- a well for the thirsty
- a testimony of God's goodness
- a living invitation to Christ

Your overflow is not just for you. It is for your family, your friends, your church, your purpose, and your generation.

Overflow is evangelism.
Overflow is ministry.
Overflow is legacy.

WHY THIS BOOK? WHY NOW?

We live in a time when:

- people are busy but empty
- connected but lonely
- full of information but starving for wisdom
- successful but unfulfilled
- spiritually active but spiritually drained

Christians have never been more engaged ... and never felt more depleted.

God is calling His people back to fullness—back to abiding, healing, wholeness, joy, and overflow.

This book is an invitation to experience all God intended.

WHAT THIS BOOK WILL HELP YOU DO

By the time you finish these pages, you will know:

- what keeps you empty
- what God wants to pour into you
- how to repair the leaks in your soul

- how to build rhythms that keep you full
- how to cultivate a life of consistent overflow
- how to become a vessel God can pour through to others

Overflow is possible.
Overflow is promised.
Overflow is your inheritance in Christ.

And it begins with this simple truth:

You are the container.
God is the source.
What you pour in determines what overflows out.

Welcome to the journey.
Let's build the life God can fill—the life that spills over—the life that touches the world.

CHAPTER 1

The Promise of Overflow

"My joy will overflow" (John 15:11).

There are moments in Scripture where Jesus pulls back the curtain and lets us see directly into His heart—moments when He reveals not just what He expects from us, but what He desires *for* us. John 15 is one of those moments. It is the final night of Jesus' earthly ministry before His arrest. It is the last extended teaching He gives His disciples before the cross. He knows His time is short. He knows they are afraid. He knows confusion and sorrow are waiting outside the door.

And in that sacred upper room, Jesus offers a surprising promise—not of survival, not of endurance, not of faith under pressure … but of **joy**.

Overflowing joy.

Not the thin joy of circumstances.
Not the fragile joy of emotion.
Not the temporary joy of accomplishment.
But **His joy**—the joy of Christ Himself.

> **"I have told you these things so that you will be filled with my joy. Yes, your joy will overflow" (John 15:11, NLT).**

Overflow.
More than enough.
Beyond capacity.
Spilling over.

Jesus is not speaking poetically.
He is speaking **prophetically**.
He is describing the normal Christian life—life *in Him*.

But if we're honest … many of us do not live with overflowing joy.

We live with:

- occasional joy
- conditional joy
- fragile joy
- leaking joy
- borrowed joy
- momentary joy
- "when things calm down" joy

This gap between what Jesus promised and what many believers experience is where this entire book begins.

WHY DID JESUS TALK ABOUT OVERFLOW ON HIS MOST DIFFICULT NIGHT?

Because He wanted His disciples to understand that the life He offers is not dependent on external peace, but internal presence. Not dependent on life going well, but on life being rooted in the Vine. Not dependent on circumstances changing, but on *them* changing.

Overflow is not the result of a perfect life.
Overflow is the result of a connected life.

THE CONTEXT OF THE PROMISE

To understand the promise of overflow, we must understand the conversation in John 15. Jesus is teaching His disciples about the Vine and the branches. He describes:

- **the Father as the Gardener**
- **Himself as the true Vine**
- **us as the branches**

The image is simple but profound:

A branch does not produce by effort; it produces by connection.
A branch does not overflow by striving; it overflows by abiding.

Everything Jesus says in this chapter revolves around one word: **remain** (or abide).
Remain in Me.
Remain in My love.
Remain in My Word.
Remain connected.

Why?
Because He knows this:

Disconnected branches don't overflow; they dry out.
But connected branches bear fruit—much fruit—lasting fruit.

OVERFLOW IS NOT A LUXURY—IT IS A KINGDOM PROMISE

Many Christians view joy as an optional bonus—nice when it comes, but not essential. Yet Jesus speaks of joy as central to the Christian life.

Jesus speaks of:

- Fullness
- Abundance
- Fruitfulness
- Overflow

Think of Psalm 23: "My cup **overflows**." This is not poetic exaggeration. David is describing a spiritual reality: **God fills to the point of spilling.**

Or consider Romans 15:13: "May the God of hope fill you with all joy and peace … so that you may overflow with hope by the power of the Holy Spirit."

Paul uses the same language Jesus used. Overflow is the work of the Spirit, not the work of human effort. But the clearest promise is still Jesus' own: **"My joy in you … your joy overflowing."** This is not motivational. This is the divine intention for your life.

The first miracle Jesus performed was not survival—it was overflow. At a wedding in Cana, when the wine ran out, Jesus turned water into wine. Not a small amount, but roughly 150 gallons. The Kingdom begins with abundance. John 10:10: "I have come that they may have life, and have it abundantly."

OVERFLOW BEGINS WITH "THESE THINGS"

Jesus does not promise overflow in a vacuum. He says: **"I have told you these things so that …"**

So what are "these things"?

Everything He taught in John 15:

- Abide in Me.
- Let My Word remain in you.
- Allow the Father to prune you.
- Remain in My love.
- Keep My commandments.
- Love one another.

These are the conditions of overflow. Not legalistic conditions—**relational conditions**.

Joy is the fruit of abiding.
Overflow is the harvest of surrender.

Jesus is teaching that joy is not an emotion we chase; it is a result of connection.

If we remain in Him, joy will come. It must come. It cannot not come. It is the fruit of the Vine flowing into the branch.

OVERFLOW IS NOT ABOUT HAPPINESS—IT IS ABOUT WHOLENESS

Many believers confuse joy with happiness.
But happiness is external; joy is internal.
Happiness is seasonal; joy is spiritual.
Happiness is based on what happens; joy is based on Who indwells.

Happiness evaporates when life is difficult.
Joy deepens in difficulty.
Happiness ends when circumstances change.
Joy expands when Christ remains.

Jesus is not offering happy moments.
He is offering **a joyful identity**.

Joy is not a mood; it is a mark of spiritual health.
Joy is not the absence of pain; it is the presence of Christ.
Joy is not a feeling; it is a fruit.

> **I have come that they may have life, and have it abundantly" (John 10:10).**
>
> **"In your presence there is fullness of joy" (Psalm 16:11).**
>
> **The kingdom of God is righteousness, peace and joy in the Holy Spirit" (Romans 14:17).**

Biblical joy is not merely emotional happiness; it is the settled assurance that God is present and faithful. This joy flows from communion with Christ and is sustained by the Holy Spirit.

> **"Though the fig tree does not bud … yet I will rejoice in the Lord" (Habakkuk 3:17–18).**

This reinforces that **joy is independent of circumstances**.

Overflow happens when you are so connected to the life of Christ that His life becomes your life, His joy becomes your joy, His strength becomes your strength.

OVERFLOW IS CONTAGIOUS

Overflow does not stop with you.
It spills.

It pours.
It touches.

People with overflowing joy:

- lift burdens
- strengthen the weary
- encourage the discouraged
- bless without trying
- radiate peace
- shift atmospheres
- ignite hope
- draw others to Christ

The world is starving for joy—not entertainment, not noise, not distraction—**joy**.

Overflow is evangelistic. People are drawn to the Christ they see flowing out of you.

We often focus on how we can reach others. Jesus focuses on what we must become.

Become full.
Become healed.
Become connected.
Become whole.

Then you will overflow, and your overflow will touch the world.

OVERFLOW IS THE RESULT OF FORMATION, NOT PERFORMANCE

Jesus never commands the disciples to produce joy. He commands them to abide.

Joy is not commanded; joy is promised.
Jesus does not say, "Work hard and be joyful."
He says, "Remain in Me … and joy will overflow."

This shifts everything.

The question is not: "How do I get more joy?" The question is: "How do I remain more deeply in Christ?"

The issue is not your effort, but your connection. Not your striving, but your surrender. Not your performance, but your posture.

Overflow comes when your life becomes a vessel—whole, open, aligned, abiding.

THE INVITATION

In the chapters ahead, we will explore:

- the condition of your container
- the leaks that drain joy
- the things God pours into your life
- the practices that build capacity
- and the pathway to consistent, abundant overflow

But before we go any further, you must settle this truth in your heart:

Overflow is God's desire for you.
You were made for fullness, not emptiness.
You were created to spill over, not dry out.
You were designed to be a vessel of joy.

Jesus has already made the promise. The question now is whether you will become the container He can fill.

This is the promise of overflow.
This is the life you were made for.
And this is the journey we are about to begin.

REFLECTION

1. What does "overflowing joy" mean to you personally?

2. Where do you see a gap between the joy Jesus promised and the joy you currently experience?

3. Which part of John 15 speaks most deeply to your current season?

____
____
____
____
____
____
____
____
____

4. What distracts you from abiding consistently in Christ?

____
____
____
____
____
____
____
____

5. What would your life look like if you truly lived in overflow?

____
____
____
____
____
____
____
____

CHAPTER 2

The Vessel God Uses

God created you as a vessel.

Before you ever took your first breath, before a single day unfolded in your story, before you made mistakes or experienced wounds—God intentionally designed you to carry something sacred.

You are not random clay.
You are chosen clay.
Formed, shaped, and purposed by the Potter.

Paul writes:

> **"We now have this light shining in our hearts, but we ourselves are like fragile clay jars containing this great treasure" (2 Corinthians 4:7, NLT).**

This simple image is stunning.

God places the treasure of His presence inside the fragility of human vessels. This means:

- God is not surprised by your limits.
- God is not intimidated by your humanity.
- God is not hindered by your weaknesses.

- God knows exactly what He placed His treasure into—and He still chose you.

Because the power is not in the clay. The power is in the One who fills the clay.

1. GOD USES VESSELS—NOT PERFORMERS, NOT PROFESSIONALS, NOT THE PERFECT

Throughout Scripture, God consistently chooses **vessels**:

- Vessel-like shepherds (David)
- Vessel-like fishermen (the disciples)
- Vessel-like mothers (Hannah, Mary)
- Vessel-like exiles (Daniel, Esther)
- Vessel-like servants (Ruth)
- Vessel-like prophets (Jeremiah, Ezekiel)

Not once did God search for perfection. He searched for vessels. He is still searching today.

Paul told Timothy: **"If you keep yourself pure, you will be a special utensil for honorable use … ready for the Master to use for every good work" (2 Timothy 2:21, NLT).**

God doesn't ask for perfection.
He asks for **purity → availability → readiness**.

He is looking for:

- vessels He can fill
- vessels He can send
- vessels He can sustain
- vessels He can overflow through

2. A VESSEL IS DEFINED BY WHAT IT CARRIES, NOT WHAT IT'S MADE OF

A clay jar is ordinary until something extraordinary is placed inside it.

Your value is not defined by:

- your achievements
- your education
- your background
- your failures
- your broken places
- your skill
- your personality

Your value is defined by **what you carry**.

And you carry:

- the Spirit of God
- the Word of God
- the love of Christ
- the light of heaven
- the hope of glory
- the fruit of the Spirit
- the presence of Jesus

You are a vessel of the supernatural.

3. THE POTTER SHAPES THE VESSEL ACCORDING TO PURPOSE

Jeremiah gives us a vivid prophetic image:

> **"But the jar he was making did not turn out as he had hoped, so he crushed it into a lump of clay again and started over" (Jeremiah 18:4, NLT).**

The Potter does not discard clay that collapses.
He reshapes it.
He reforms it.
He starts over—not because the clay is worthless, but because the Potter has a vision for it.

> **"Yet you, LORD, are our Father. We are the clay, you are the potter; we are all the work of your hand" (Isaiah 64:8).**

Your life is not shaped by accidents. Your story is shaped by hands. The Potter's hands. He shapes you according to **purpose**, not preference. The purpose determines the design.

A drinking cup is shaped differently than a water jar.
A water jar is shaped differently than a lamp.
A lamp is shaped differently than a bowl.

In the same way:

Your calling shapes your capacity.
Your purpose shapes your formation.
Your assignment shapes your process.

God knows what He's forming you for—even when you don't. Scripture consistently portrays God as the divine Potter shaping the lives of His people. Our formation is not accidental; it is intentional craftsmanship. God forms each believer uniquely so that the life of Christ may be expressed through them in a particular way.

4. AN EFFECTIVE VESSEL MUST BE: WHOLE, CLEAN, AND AVAILABLE

A vessel is simple. But it has requirements.

A. A Vessel Must Be Whole

A cracked vessel cannot hold liquid. It may appear beautiful externally, but it is structurally compromised. This is why God begins with healing. He heals:

- the cracks of trauma
- the cracks of disappointment
- the cracks of sin
- the cracks of shame
- the cracks of neglect

Before God uses you greatly, He restores you deeply.

B. A Vessel Must Be Clean

In biblical times, vessels used for sacred purposes had to be washed, purified, and set apart. God still desires clean vessels today:

vessels free from the residue of past sin,
vessels not filled with yesterday's bitterness,
vessels emptied of pride, fear, shame, self-reliance, and clutter.

Psalm 51:10 says: **"Create in me a clean heart, O God."**

A clean heart becomes a ready vessel.

C. A Vessel Must Be Available

The greatest ability in the Kingdom is **availability**. Isaiah said: **"Here I am. Send me!"** (Isaiah 6:8). God does not ask:

"Are you talented?"
"Are you experienced?"
"Are you impressive?"

He asks:
"Are you available?"

A vessel cannot be filled or used if it remains hidden on a shelf.

BIBLICAL STORY ILLUSTRATION

Gideon (Judges 6)

God used:

a fearful man
hiding in a winepress
questioning God

Yet God called him: "Mighty warrior." God does not look for impressive vessels—He looks for available ones.

5. A VESSEL SET APART FOR PURPOSE

In the Old Testament, some vessels were kept for common use—ordinary, everyday, functional.

Others were set apart for holy use—dedicated, protected, purified, sacred.

Paul picks up this language: **"In a great house there are vessels of gold and silver … some for honorable use, some for common use"** (2 Timothy 2:20).

The difference is not in the clay. The difference is in the **consecration**. When you choose to set yourself apart for God, He sets apart His purposes for you. When you choose consecration, God chooses increase. When you choose purity, God chooses power.

6. ILLUSTRATION: THE VESSEL IN THE POTTER'S HOUSE

Imagine walking into a potter's workshop. On one shelf sits a cracked, dusty vessel—ignored, unused, forgotten. Nearby sits a beautiful vessel, restored, strengthened, glazed, and ready.

Same clay.
Same potter.
Different conditions.

Now imagine your life on that shelf. Which vessel are you becoming? The Potter is not scanning the room for perfect clay. He is searching for clay willing to be shaped.

7. BEFORE GOD FILLS YOU, HE FORMS YOU

You cannot skip formation. You cannot bypass preparation.

God forms your:

- character
- integrity
- humility
- emotional maturity
- spiritual stability
- inner strength
- capacity

Overflow requires structure. The deeper the roots, the greater the fruit. The stronger the container, the greater the outpouring. God loves you too much to fill a vessel that will break under the weight of what He pours. So, He forms you first.

8. THE INVITATION OF THIS CHAPTER

God is not only asking: "Do you want overflow?" He is asking: "Do you want to be the kind of vessel I can overflow through?"

This chapter invites you to ask:

- Am I whole?
- Am I clean?
- Am I available?
- Am I surrendered?
- Am I formed or merely functional?
- Am I ready for the purpose God has for me?

Because here is the truth:

Overflow is about the vessel you become.

And you—yes, you—are a vessel God is forming for something glorious.

REFLECTION

1. How do you see yourself—as a vessel? What emotions arise with this metaphor?

2. What do you believe God created you to carry?

3. Which characteristics of a suitable vessel (whole, clean, empty, available, set apart) challenge you the most?

4. What areas of your life feel ready for God to fill?

5. Where do you sense God preparing or reshaping you right now?

CHAPTER 3

When the Container Is Cracked

There is a kind of brokenness that does not shout. A kind that does not bleed.

A kind that cannot be seen from the outside—yet quietly drains a person from the inside. It is the hidden crack. And every believer, no matter how strong, no matter how anointed, no matter how sincere, carries cracks in their container. These cracks are not signs of failure. They are signs of humanity. They are reminders that we were made from clay—fragile, formable, and dependent on a Potter.

Paul understood this deeply: **"We have this treasure in jars of clay, to show that this all-surpassing power is from God and not from us"** (2 Corinthians 4:7).

Jars of clay crack.
Jars of clay leak.
Jars of clay break under pressure.

But the treasure inside the jar does not diminish because of the jar's condition. The treasure remains glorious. What needs healing is not the treasure—but the vessel.

1. PRESSURE REVEALS CRACKS, IT DOESN'T CREATE THEM

Life has a way of exposing weaknesses we didn't know we had:

- a harsh comment that cuts deeper than it should
- an unexpected disappointment that shatters confidence
- a season of stretching that reveals impatience
- a betrayal that exposes fear
- a loss that surfaces grief we didn't know was buried

Pressure is like fire—it reveals what is inside the vessel and exposes the fault lines beneath the glaze. Consider Peter. He sincerely loved Jesus. He said boldly: **"Even if everyone else deserts you, I will never desert you"** (Matthew 26:33).

But under pressure—the pressure of fear, danger, and scrutiny—a crack appeared. Peter denied Jesus three times. His crack was not a lack of love. It was an unhealed fear. Pressure didn't create it; it revealed it. Your cracks may be:

- insecurity
- rejection
- past trauma
- fear of failure
- fear of abandonment
- unhealed grief
- hidden sin
- unaddressed disappointment
- childhood wounds
- unforgiveness

All of these create openings where joy leaks. You may not notice the crack immediately—but you will notice the drain.

2. CRACKS ARE FORMED IN THE SECRET PLACES

Cracks don't appear during revival moments. They appear during silent seasons.

- A harsh word from childhood that still echoes
- A betrayal that built a wall
- A sin you tried to bury instead of heal
- A prayer that wasn't answered the way you hoped
- A person who left without explanation
- A success that filled you with quiet pride
- A failure that filled you with quiet shame

Some cracks were inherited from family patterns. Some cracks were formed by trauma. Some cracks formed through gradual drift—a slow erosion of the soul. But every crack tells a story. And God wants to heal everyone. He does not shame the cracked vessel. He restores it.

3. THE DANGER OF IGNORED CRACKS

When cracks are left unaddressed, they become leaks. A leaking vessel is:

- always tired
- always spiritually empty
- always starting over
- always trying harder with little progress
- always feeling "almost full" but never overflowing

You might think:

"I just need more prayer."
"I just need more worship."
"I just need more sermons."

But without healing, the more God pours … the more will leak out. This is why people experience:

- great worship on Sunday
- emptiness by Wednesday
- spiritual highs that fade quickly
- joy that lasts only moments
- peace that evaporates under stress

The problem isn't the pouring. It's the leaking.

4. THE POTTER NEVER DISCARDS A CRACKED VESSEL

In Jeremiah 18, God gives the prophet a vision: **"The vessel he was shaping from the clay was marred in his hands; so the potter formed it into another vessel, shaping it as seemed best to him"** (Jeremiah 18:4, KJV).

Notice what the Potter did NOT do:

- He did not throw the clay away.
- He did not get angry at the clay.
- He did not label the clay "defective."
- He did not shame the clay for being marred.

He simply reshaped it. The Potter only does two things with damaged clay:

- He holds it.
- He reforms it.

You may feel marred. You may feel cracked. You may feel like the container of your life is too weak to hold joy. But the Potter is holding you. He is shaping you according to His vision for your future—not your past. Cracks do not disqualify you. Cracks prepare you for divine restoration.

5. GOD HEALS CRACKS THROUGH TRUTH, PRESENCE, AND PROCESS

A. Truth Exposes the Crack

Scripture is a mirror. **"Your word is a lamp to my feet and a light to my path"** (Psalm 119:105).

Light reveals what darkness hides. Sometimes God will show you a crack through:

- conviction
- a Scripture passage
- a sermon
- a conversation
- a moment of reflection

Truth does not expose to condemn. Truth exposes to heal.

B. Presence Softens the Clay

Clay becomes flexible in the hands of the potter when it is wet. In the same way, you become formable in the presence of God. Healing rarely comes through willpower. It comes through **presence—His nearness, His Spirit, His love.**

David said: **"He restores my soul"** (Psalm 23:3). Restoration happens in the presence of the Shepherd.

C. Process Seals the Crack

Healing is often gradual:

- forgiveness
- counseling
- spiritual practices
- confession
- healthy relationships
- new habits
- rest
- prayer

Healing is not instant formation. Healing is long obedience in the same direction. The Potter shapes slowly, intentionally, masterfully—because the vessel He is forming must be able to endure the weight of glory He plans to pour into it.

6. THE ILLUSTRATION: THE JAPANESE ART OF KINTSUGI

There is a Japanese art form called **kintsugi**, meaning "golden repair."

When a ceramic vessel cracks or breaks, instead of throwing it away, artisans repair it with resin mixed with gold dust. The cracks are not hidden—they are highlighted with gold. The repaired vessel is considered **more valuable** than before it was broken. This is the Gospel in art form. God does not simply patch your cracks—He fills them with glory.

Your healed wounds carry wisdom.
Your restored places shine with grace.
Your past pain becomes future ministry.
Your cracks, filled with divine gold, become the most beautiful part of your testimony.
Where you were broken, you become radiant.

This is the promise: "**My power works best in weakness**" (2 Corinthians 12:9).

The crack becomes the place where grace flows.

7. HEALING CRACKS EXPANDS CAPACITY

A healed vessel can hold more than before.

Your capacity for joy increases.
Your ability to receive increases.
Your resilience strengthens.
Your empathy deepens.
Your emotional bandwidth widens.
Your spiritual authority grows.

The enemy cracks your container to weaken you. God heals your container to enlarge you.

8. THE INVITATION TO BE HEALED

This chapter is not an accusation. It is an invitation. God is asking:

- Will you let Me show you the cracks?
- Will you let Me restore what has drained you?
- Will you let Me heal what life broke?
- Will you let Me strengthen what pressure exposed?
- Will you let Me reform you into the vessel I see?

The Potter is ready. **Jacob Wrestles with God – Genesis 32.** Jacob leaves that encounter **with a limp**. Meaning: God heals and transforms but sometimes leaves a mark of humility. Quote:

"Your name will no longer be Jacob, but Israel…" (Genesis 32:28). Brokenness is a means that He uses to **produce transformation**.

He is patient with your process.
He is tender with your wounds.
He is faithful with your formation.

Your cracks do not scare Him.
Your weakness does not offend Him.
Your brokenness does not disappoint Him.

He loves you too much to leave you leaking. And He is ready to heal your container.

Overflow begins here.

REFLECTION

1. What cracks or weaknesses has God been gently revealing in this season?

2. How have these cracks affected your ability to hold joy or peace?

3. Which cracks have you tried to hide rather than heal?

4. In what ways has pressure revealed underlying issues in your heart?

5. How does knowing God as the Potter who restores, change how you view your broken places?

CHAPTER 4

The Leak of Unhealed Wounds

Some wounds bleed on the surface. But others bleed in the soul.

There are wounds you can point to—and wounds you can barely name.
There are wounds time has covered—but never healed.
There are wounds you've learned to function with—but not flourish through.

There is a kind of pain that doesn't bleed but still breaks. A kind of wound no one sees but God. A kind of hurt that hides beneath the surface—quiet, deep, unspoken—that silently drains the soul. Every believer carries wounds from life in a fallen world.

Wounds from childhood.
Wounds from relationships.
Wounds from betrayal or disappointment.
Wounds from failure.
Wounds from people who should have protected us but didn't.
Wounds from moments we wish we could forget.

And unless those wounds are healed, they become cracks—openings through which joy leaks, peace drains, and strength dissipates.

Unhealed wounds are one of the greatest thieves of spiritual overflow. And every unhealed wound creates a leak. You don't have to feel pain for that wound to drain you. It may be silent. It may be buried. But it drains you nonetheless.

It drains joy.
It drains hope.
It drains confidence.
It drains peace.
It drains emotional strength.
It drains spiritual vitality.

Unhealed wounds are cracks the enemy exploits.

1. TIME DOES NOT HEAL ALL WOUNDS—JESUS DOES

People say: "Just give it time." But time itself does not heal—it only reveals. Time may:

- soothe the pain
- soften the sting
- distance the memory

But only **Jesus heals**. He declared His mission this way: **"He has sent Me to heal the brokenhearted"** (Luke 4:18, NKJV).

Not judge the brokenhearted. Not ignore the brokenhearted. Not tell the brokenhearted to "move on." But **heal** them. This one verse reveals the heart of Jesus toward your wounds.

He does not rush your healing.
He does not dismiss your feelings.
He does not shame your tears.
He bends toward the broken places.
He binds. He restores. He repairs.

Whatever wounded you, Jesus came for that. Broken hearts do not heal themselves. They need a Healer. The Greek word for "brokenhearted" means: **"Shattered into pieces."**

Jesus came for the shattered.
He came for the bruised.
He came for the bleeding places no one sees.

He came for you.

2. UNHEALED WOUNDS BECOME EMOTIONAL LEAKS

A wound not healed becomes a weakness in the vessel.

Hidden wounds often show up as:

- a short temper
- overreaction to stress
- distrust of people
- difficulty receiving love
- feeling "not enough"
- sudden emotional shutdown
- fear of intimacy
- self-sabotage
- chronic anxiety
- the inability to rest

These are not personality traits—they are signals. They are symptoms of deeper cracks. Joy does not simply disappear; it is drained. Unhealed wounds:

- create emotional instability
- amplify negative thoughts
- distort your view of God
- make relationships difficult

- steal spiritual confidence
- hinder prayer
- weaken your sense of identity
- make love hard to give or receive
- drain your ability to rest

You can be pouring in the Word, prayer, worship, and community—but if the wound is open, it silently empties everything God is trying to fill. Healing closes the leak.

God reveals these not to overwhelm you, but to invite you into deeper wholeness. He wants to heal the cause, not just manage the symptoms. Sometimes that weakness is:

A. Emotional

- bitterness
- resentment
- sadness
- insecurity
- low self-worth
- defensiveness

B. Behavioral

- withdrawal
- overcompensation
- perfectionism
- self-sabotage
- avoidance
- people-pleasing

C. Spiritual

- inconsistent devotion
- difficulty trusting God

- feeling numb toward worship
- feeling distant in prayer
- feeling unworthy of God's love

A heart that has learned to survive often has not learned to heal.

3. WOUNDS COME FROM PEOPLE—AND HEALING COMES FROM A PERSON

Most wounds come through relationships:

- a parent's criticism
- a friend's betrayal
- a spouse's indifference
- a leader's failure
- a partner's abandonment
- a childhood trauma
- a relational rupture

The human heart is wounded by people—but healed by one Person. Though each person's story is unique, certain categories of wounds appear again and again:

A. Family Wounds

Homes filled with conflict, neglect, comparison, criticism, or absence shape the soul.

B. Relationship Wounds

Rejection, betrayal, abandonment, divorce, manipulation, or abuse create deep fractures.

C. Church Wounds

Spiritual manipulation, harsh leadership, hypocrisy, exclusion, or misunderstanding leave invisible scars.

D. Self-Inflicted Wounds

Failures, poor decisions, shame, guilt, and regret can become internal wounds that eat away at identity.

E. Circumstantial Wounds

Loss of a loved one, traumatic events, chronic illness, financial collapse, or dreams that died.

Every wound has a story. And every wound can be healed.

Jesus, the Restorer of Souls.

David said: **"He heals the brokenhearted and binds up their wounds"** (Psalm 147:3).

To "bind" means to wrap tightly, to attend to, to treat carefully. God is not a casual healer. He is intentional. He binds, He restores, He repairs.

4. THE WOUND YOU IGNORE WILL BECOME THE WEAKNESS YOU ACCEPT

Most believers don't deny their wounds; they minimize them. We say things like:

"I'm fine."
"It wasn't that bad."
"I've already moved on."
"That was years ago."
"I don't want to revisit it."

"I should be over this."
"I forgave them already."

But forgiveness is not the same as healing. You can forgive instantly—but healing is a **process**. You can move on from something physically—while still carrying it emotionally. Ignoring wounds is not strength. It is slow draining.

5. GOD DOESN'T HEAL WHAT YOU HIDE

God heals what you reveal. Not because He doesn't know—but because humility releases His touch. David said: **"Search me, O God, and know my heart; test me … point out anything in me that offends You"** (Psalm 139:23–24).

This is a prayer for exposure. Not exposure to shame. Exposure to heal. Healing begins where honesty begins.

6. THE SAMARITAN WOMAN: A WOUND COVERED IN SHAME

In John 4, the Samaritan woman came to draw water at noon—the hottest part of the day.

Why?

Because shame is a wound that avoids people. She had relational wounds, identity wounds, rejection wounds—and she hid them. But Jesus met her there. He gently revealed the truth she had buried … not to expose her shame, but to free her from it. He turned her wound into her witness. The first evangelist in Samaria was a wounded woman healed by Jesus. Your healed wound will become a testimony that overflows.

7. HOW GOD HEALS DEEP WOUNDS

A. He Brings Truth to Lies

Every wound carries a lie:

"I'm unwanted."
"I'm unlovable."
"I'm invisible."
"I'm defective."
"I'm alone."
"I'm not enough."

Truth disarms lies.

> **"You will know the truth, and the truth will set you free" (John 8:32).**

B. He Brings Presence to Pain

Healing happens in His nearness.

> **"He is close to the brokenhearted" (Psalm 34:18).**

> **"By his wounds we are healed" (Isaiah 53:5).**

God does His best work in broken places.

C. He Brings People to Walk with You

God often heals through community—counseling, friendships, mentors, pastors.

D. He Brings Purpose Out of Pain

Wounds healed become wisdom.
Pain redeemed becomes purpose.

Joseph's Wounds – Genesis 37–50

Joseph experienced:

- betrayal by brothers
- slavery
- false accusation
- prison

Yet he later says: "You meant evil against me, but God meant it for good" (Genesis 50:20).

God does not waste your wounds.

8. THE INVITATION TO HEALING

You are not weak because you have wounds. You are human. You are clay. And the Potter is not intimidated by the cracks. He is ready to heal them. Your overflow begins with healing.

REFLECTION

1. What past wound or experience still impacts you today

____

____

____

____

____

____

____

____

____

____

2. How have you seen unhealed pain leak into your emotions, relationships, or habits?

3. What emotions or memories do you avoid bringing to God?

4. How has the Holy Spirit been nudging you toward healing?

5. What would it feel like to give God full access to your deepest wound?

CHAPTER 5

The Leak of Unconfessed Sin

There is a kind of leaking that does not come from pain—it comes from **distance**. Distance from God created by sin. Sin is not an embarrassing mistake. Sin is not a flaw to manage. Sin is not simply "falling short."

Sin is a **fracture** in the vessel. A break in the bond. A crack in the container. Sin creates spiritual leakage. Not because God stops pouring but because sin opens a gap where joy drains.

1. SIN IS THE ENEMY OF OVERFLOW

David understood this intimately. After his sin with Bathsheba, he prayed: **"Restore to me the joy of your salvation"** (Psalm 51:12). He didn't say: "Restore my salvation." He said: "Restore my **joy**." Sin not only removes salvation—but it also steals joy.

Sin fogs clarity.
Sin dulls spiritual hunger.
Sin dims passion.
Sin hinders worship.

Sin steals confidence.
Sin damages capacity.
Sin is a leak.

2. HIDDEN SIN IS HEAVY SIN

David wrote: "**When I kept silent, my bones wasted away … my strength evaporated like water in the summer heat"** (Psalm 32:3–4, NLT).

Silence is suffocating.
Secrecy is draining.
Shame is heavy.

The most exhausting life is the life lived in the shadows. Every hidden sin demands emotional energy to maintain it:

- lying
- pretending
- managing image
- avoiding
- self-justifying
- numbing

Covering sin drains more than committing sin. Think of Achan in Joshua 7 who attempted to hide his sins. That hidden sin caused defeat for the entire nation. Hidden sin drains spiritual power.

3. CONFESSION IS NOT EXPOSURE—IT IS FREEDOM

The enemy whispers:

"If anyone knew, they would reject you."
"If God knew, He would punish you."
"If you confess, you'll be disqualified."

But confession is not condemnation. Confession is cleansing. John declares: **"If we confess our sins, He is faithful and just to forgive us our sins and to cleanse us from all unrighteousness"** (1 John 1:9).

Mold hidden behind a wall keeps spreading until the wall is opened. Confession is opening the wall. "Then I acknowledged my sin to you … and you forgave the guilt of my sin" (Psalm 32:5).

Confession restores connection.
Confession stops the leak.
Confession brings light.
Confession brings freedom.

Confession is not God shaming you. It is God washing you.

4. THE PRODIGAL—SIN BREAKS JOY BEFORE IT BREAKS ANYTHING ELSE

The prodigal son did not lose his identity; he was still a son; he lost his joy.

He spent recklessly.
He lost everything.
He hit rock bottom.

But the moment he confessed: "**Father, I have sinned …** " (Luke 15:21).

Something shifted. He was restored, honored, embraced, and celebrated. Confession didn't demote him. It restored him. Confession closes leaks. Confession welcomes overflow.

5. THE PURPOSE OF CONVICTION

Conviction is not God pointing out your flaws. Conviction is God pointing you back to Himself. Conviction is love. Conviction is rescue. Conviction is protection.

Romans 2:4 says: **"The kindness of God leads you to repentance."** Repentance is not punishment. It is the path back to joy.

6. HOW TO HEAL THE LEAK OF SIN

A. Be Honest with God

He knows already—but honesty aligns your heart with His.

B. Be Honest with Someone Safe

James 5:16 says: **"Confess your sins to one another and pray for one another, so that you may be healed."** Forgiveness comes from God. Healing often comes through community.

C. Replace Lies with Truth

Every sin has a root lie. Expose it. Replace it with Scripture.

D. Build Habits That Protect Your Heart

Sin leaks where discipline is weak.

7. REPENTANCE CREATES ROOM FOR OVERFLOW

Repentance is not turning from sin; it is turning toward God. It restores:

- clarity
- passion
- peace
- spiritual desire
- joy

Repentance is a return to overflow.

REFLECTION

1. Are there areas of sin you have minimized, hidden, or justified?

2. What prevents you from practicing honest confession before God?

3. How have you experienced the difference between life with unconfessed sin and life with a cleansed heart?

4. What does repentance look like for you today—not as punishment, but as restoration?

5. How might confession reopen the flow of joy in your life?

CHAPTER 6

The Leak of Unhealthy Habits and Spiritual Neglect

No container, no matter how beautifully made, can hold water if it is consistently left unattended.

Neglect creates cracks.
Neglect creates weakness.
Neglect creates leaks.

Most believers do not fall because of one catastrophic choice—they fall because of a thousand small ones. Neglect is slow leakage.

1. HABITS DETERMINE CAPACITY

Your life is shaped by what you repeatedly do. Not what you occasionally desire.

Not what you sometimes remember. Not what you theoretically value. Habits form the shape of your vessel. Jesus Himself lived by spiritual habits:

- He withdrew to pray
- He rose early to seek the Father
- He attended synagogue regularly
- He fasted
- He observed rhythms of rest

If the Son of God needed habits, so do we.

DANIEL WAS A MAN WITH STRONG HABITS – DANIEL 6

Daniel prayed **three times daily**. Even under threat, his habits sustained him.

2. THE DANGER OF SPIRITUAL NEGLECT

Neglect creates leaks in subtle ways:

- skipping time in Scripture
- going long seasons without prayer
- attending church sporadically
- replacing communion with entertainment
- letting busyness suffocate devotion
- allowing distraction to rule the mind

Neglect shrinks your capacity.
Neglect weakens your container.
Neglect makes you vulnerable to temptation.
Neglect disconnects you from the Source.

Hebrews warns: **"We must pay more careful attention … so that we do not drift away"** (Hebrews 2:1).

Drift is quiet.
Drift is gradual.
Drift is dangerous.

3. YOUR DAILY HABITS EITHER REINFORCE OR ERODE YOUR VESSEL

Habits That Reinforce

- Bible reading
- prayer
- silence
- worship
- gratitude
- fasting
- fellowship
- Sabbath
- service

Habits That Erode

- constant scrolling
- unchecked entertainment
- unhealthy relationships
- complaining
- overworking
- isolation
- ignoring emotional health

Nothing drains as quietly as distraction.

4. THE ILLUSTRATION: THE NEGLECTED GARDEN

A garden never becomes beautiful by accident. If you leave a garden unattended:

- weeds grow
- soil hardens
- pests come
- fruit dies

Neglect invites decay.

Likewise, your spiritual life is a garden. It must be tended:

Watered.
Weeded.
Guarded.
Cultivated.

A neglected garden cannot produce fruit; and a neglected soul cannot produce overflow.

5. SPIRITUAL HABITS ARE NOT LEGALISM; THEY ARE LIFELINES

We confuse discipline with legalism. But they are not the same. Legalism says: "I must do this so God will accept me." Discipline says: "I do this because God loves me." Habits are not about earning grace. Habits are about receiving it consistently.

6. SMALL HABITS CREATE DEEP TRANSFORMATION

Never underestimate the power of:

- 10 minutes in Scripture
- 5 minutes of prayer
- 3 minutes of gratitude
- 1 chapter of Proverbs
- one verse repeated all day
- one worship song in the morning

Small habits strengthen the vessel.
Small habits compound over time.
Small habits create sustainable overflow.

"Train yourself to be godly" (1 Timothy 4:7–8).

7. PRIORITIZING YOUR CONTAINER

Ask yourself:

- What habits weaken me?
- What rhythms strengthen me?
- What practices fill me?
- What practices drain me?
- What needs to be removed?
- What needs to be added?

Your overflow tomorrow depends on your habits today.

8. THE INVITATION

God is not asking for perfection. He is asking for partnership. Strengthening your container is not striving; it is stewardship.

The Spirit will empower you.
The Father will guide you.
Jesus will walk with you.

But you must choose the habits that enable overflow.

REFLECTION

1. Which of your daily habits feel like small cracks draining your life over time?

2. How have busyness, distraction, or neglect weakened your spiritual capacity?

3. What habit do you sense God inviting you to start—or stop?

4. How would your life change if you built consistent spiritual rhythms?

5. What small daily practice could you begin today to strengthen your vessel?

CHAPTER 7

The Leak of Emotional Clutter

There is a kind of weariness that has nothing to do with physical exhaustion. A kind of heaviness that sleep cannot fix. A kind of fatigue that sits beneath the surface; draining the soul day after day. It is the weight of **emotional clutter**.

Emotional clutter is the accumulation of unprocessed feelings, unresolved stress, mental noise, inner tension, and spiritual static that occupies the space where peace should dwell.

You can be gifted, anointed, talented, and sincere—and still leak joy because your emotional world is overcrowded.

1. EMOTIONAL CLUTTER IS A SILENT LEAK

We tend to think of leaks as dramatic—big failures, major wounds, blatant sins.

But the most dangerous leaks are the quiet ones:

- the constant pressure you never talk about
- the disappointments you pretend didn't hurt

- the internal criticism that never shuts off
- the stress you've normalized
- the fear you've learned to live with
- the comparison you scroll through
- the worry you carry into every room
- the anger you push down but never resolve

These small emotional drains slowly empty the container of your life. Solomon wrote: **"Above all else, guard your heart, for everything you do flows from it"** (Proverbs 4:23).

Where does overflow come from? **Your heart.** So, when the heart is cluttered, overflow is impossible.

2. JESUS CARRIED EMOTIONS—BUT WAS NEVER CONTROLLED BY THEM

Jesus experienced:

- joy
- sadness
- anger
- grief
- compassion
- disappointment
- loneliness

Yet He lived emotionally uncluttered.

How? Scripture shows three patterns:

A. He processed Emotions in Prayer

In Gethsemane He said: **"My soul is overwhelmed with sorrow …** " (Matthew 26:38). And He brought that emotion to the Father.

B. He Practiced Solitude

Jesus withdrew often to be alone with God to declutter His inner world.

C. He Maintained Relational Boundaries

Jesus did not say yes to every demand, fix every problem, or stay accessible to every crowd. Emotional clarity is not the absence of emotion—it is the presence of **godly boundaries, prayer, and rhythm**.

3. THE MODERN SOUL IS OVERSTIMULATED AND UNDERSURRENDERED

We live in an age of:

- nonstop notifications
- endless scrolling
- constant noise
- emotional overstimulation

The psalmist said: **"I have calmed and quieted my soul"** (Psalm 131:2).

Notice: it doesn't say, "my soul was calm." It says: **"I calmed my soul."** A quiet soul is not accidental. It is intentional. Emotional clutter builds accidentally. Emotional clarity requires practice.

4. EMOTIONAL CLUTTER OFTEN COMES FROM FOUR SOURCES

A. Internal Noise

Self-criticism, overthinking, people-pleasing, anxiety, comparison.

B. External Pressure

Work deadlines, family expectations, social pressure, financial stress.

C. Unprocessed Pain

Grief, disappointment, rejection, heartbreak.

D. Spiritual Neglect

Without prayer, presence, and Scripture, your soul becomes noisy.

David said: **"When my heart is overwhelmed, lead me to the rock … "** (Psalm 61:2).

The overwhelmed heart needs a place to go.

5. ILLUSTRATION: THE CUP FULL OF STONES

Imagine a cup filled with small stones—fear, stress, exhaustion, bitterness, shame, regret. If you pour water into it, very little can be held. The problem is not the water. The problem is what is already taking up space. You cannot be filled with what God wants to give if your soul is occupied with what life has piled inside. Overflow requires **removing**, not just adding.

6. HOW GOD HEALS EMOTIONAL CLUTTER

A. Through Stillness

"Be still, and know that I am God" (Psalm 46:10).

Stillness is spiritual surgery.

B. Through Surrender

Release the burden. Drop the stones. Let go of what God never asked you to carry.

C. Through Truth

The Word declutters lies.

D. Through Prayer

Prayer is where emotions get cleaned and reordered.

E. Through Confession

Talking honestly with God and trusted people breaks emotional congestion.

F. Through Boundaries

Jesus said no. So can you.

7. YOUR HEART WAS NOT DESIGNED FOR CLUTTER—BUT FOR CHRIST

The emotional life of a believer is meant to be:

- light, not weighed down
- peaceful, not chaotic
- free, not entangled
- spacious, not crowded

Elijah Suffered from Burnout – 1 Kings 19

Elijah was:

- exhausted
- depressed
- afraid

God restores him through:

- Rest
- Food
- Presence
- Calling

Overflow requires **room**. God wants to clear the internal space so you can carry His joy.

REFLECTION

1. What emotions or mental patterns crowd your heart most often?

____

____

____

____

____

____

2. What sources of noise, pressure, or internal chaos do you need to surrender?

____

____

____

____

____

____

3. How does emotional clutter affect your ability to hear God clearly?

4. What spiritual practice helps you quiet your soul?

5. Where do you feel God inviting you into stillness or emotional healing?

CHAPTER 8

Pouring in the Word of God

Once the vessel is healed and strengthened, the first substance the Father pours into the life of a believer is **His Word**. Not because the Word is merely instructive but because the Word is **formative**.

The Word shapes the soul.
The Word renews the mind.
The Word strengthens the heart.
The Word builds capacity.
The Word anchors identity.

Every revival in Scripture, every transformation in history, every strengthening of a believer begins with the **Word of God taking root**.

1. THE WORD OF GOD IS NOT INFORMATION—IT IS NOURISHMENT

Jesus said: **"Man shall not live by bread alone, but by every word that comes from the mouth of God"** (Matthew 4:4).

Scripture is not optional. It is sustenance. A believer without Scripture is like:

- a body without food
- a tree without roots
- a lamp without oil
- a vessel without strength

The Word is your daily bread—without it you will spiritually starve.

2. THE WORD CLEANSES THE VESSEL

Jesus said: **"You are already clean because of the word I have spoken to you"** (John 15:3).

The Word:

- purifies motives
- washes thoughts
- exposes lies
- breaks deception
- renews the mind
- frees the heart

It is not possible to live in overflow while thinking thoughts God did not plant.

The Word replaces the world's noise with heaven's clarity.

3. THE WORD STRENGTHENS THE VESSEL

Psalm 119 is a masterpiece on this truth.

> **"Your word has given me life" (Psalm 119:50).**

> **"Your statutes are my counselors" (Psalm 119:24).**
>
> **"I run in the path of Your commands, for You have set my heart free" (Psalm 119:32).**
>
> **"Your word is a lamp to my feet, and a light to my path" (Psalm 119:105).**

Scripture doesn't just inform you. Scripture **stabilizes** you. A vessel filled with Scripture cannot be easily shaken.

4. THE WORD BUILDS YOUR CAPACITY TO HOLD JOY

The Word is not merely defensive; it is **expansive**. The more of the Word you internalize:

- the bigger your faith becomes
- the greater your peace becomes
- the stronger your character becomes
- the deeper your spiritual roots grow
- the larger your spiritual capacity grows

The Word enlarges the vessel. Jeremiah said: **"Your words were found, and I ate them; Your words became my joy . . . "** (Jeremiah 15:16). Joy is the fruit of consuming Scripture.

5. THE ILLUSTRATION: THE TREE PLANTED BY STREAMS

Psalm 1 describes the person saturated in Scripture: **"They are like a tree planted by streams of water ... Whatever they do prospers"** (Psalm 1:3).

A tree by water does not fear drought. A believer rooted in Scripture does not fear seasons. Because the Word creates resilience.

6. HOW TO POUR THE WORD INTO YOUR LIFE

A. Read Daily

Even a little every day builds depth.

B. Meditate Slowly

Let Scripture move from head to heart.

C. Memorize Strategically

Memorize verses for your weakest places.

D. Study Intentionally

Go deeper into themes, characters, books.

E. Speak the Word

Declare it. Pray it. Preach it to yourself.

F. Obey Immediately

Revelation without obedience creates spiritual stagnation.

7. THE WORD MAKES YOU OVERFLOW

When Scripture fills your mind:

- your words change
- your decisions change
- your reactions change
- your desires change
- your emotions change
- Overflow becomes natural.

REFLECTION

1. How has Scripture shaped your life in past seasons?

2. What obstacles keep you from engaging the Word consistently?

3. What Scripture passages have healed, strengthened, or guided you recently?

4. How could you allow the Word to "dwell richly" in you this week?

5. What new rhythm of Bible intake would deepen your capacity for overflow?

CHAPTER 9

Pouring in the Presence of God

You were created for presence.

Not for religion.
Not for ritual.
Not for routine.
Not even for spiritual disciplines alone.

You were created for **intimacy with God**. Before Adam did any work, before he named any animals, before he received any assignment, he walked with God.

Presence comes before purpose.
Intimacy comes before influence.
Connection comes before calling.

You were made to dwell.

1. PRESENCE IS THE PLACE OF FILLING

In the presence of God:

- anxiety melts
- fear dissolves
- shame lifts
- heaviness breaks
- clarity comes
- peace flows
- joy rises
- identity settles

This is why the psalmist said: **"In Your presence is fullness of joy"** (Psalm 16:11). Fullness; not survival, not partiality, not scarcity. Presence fills what nothing else can.

2. PRESENCE IS NOT AN EVENT—IT IS A LIFESTYLE

We often reduce God's presence to:

- a moment in worship
- a powerful church service
- a prayer meeting

But presence is not confined to a place. Jesus said: **"I am with you always"** (Matthew 28:20).

Presence is continuous.
Presence is relational.
Presence is internal.

God is not someone you visit. God is someone you abide with.

3. THE DIFFERENCE BETWEEN VISITING AND ABIDING

Many believers **visit** God. Few believers **abide** in God.

Visiting produces inspiration. Abiding produces transformation.

Visiting fills temporarily. Abiding fills continually.

Visiting creates moments. Abiding creates overflow.

Jesus says: **"Remain in Me … apart from Me you can do nothing"** (John 15:4–5).

The life of God flows in the abiding.

4. ABIDING REQUIRES AWARENESS

God is always present. But you are not always aware. Awareness turns proximity into intimacy. Practices that increase awareness:

- silence
- stillness
- breath prayer
- gratitude
- listening
- slowing down
- Scripture meditation
- fasting
- rest
- journaling

These practices clear space for presence.

5. GOD'S PRESENCE HEALS WHAT ENERGY CANNOT FIX

Many believers try to solve spiritual problems with:

- more effort
- more discipline

- more commitment
- more striving

But some things do not change with effort—they change with presence. The woman with the issue of blood touched His garment and was healed. One moment in His presence changed what twelve years of doctors could not. One moment can do what years of striving cannot.

6. THE PRESENCE OF GOD IS YOUR ENVIRONMENT

Fish require water.
Plants require light.
Humans require oxygen.
Believers require presence.

Outside of presence, you suffocate spiritually. In presence, you flourish. Moses understood this when he prayed: **"If Your Presence does not go with us, do not send us up from here"** (Exodus 33:15). He was saying: **"Your Presence is the only environment where we can thrive."**

7. THE ILLUSTRATION—THE BRANCH AND THE VINE

A branch detached from the vine cannot produce fruit—not because it stops trying, but because it loses connection. Presence is spiritual oxygen. Abiding is spiritual breathing. Without presence, we wither. With Presence, we overflow.

8. HOW TO CULTIVATE A LIFE OF PRESENCE

A. Begin Your Day with God

Offer the first moments of your morning.

B. Practice Breath Prayer

Inhale: "Lord Jesus … "
Exhale: " … have mercy on me."

C. Pause Often

Short pauses anchor your heart.

D. Invite God into Your Activities

Work, commute, parenting, chores.

E. Create Quiet Space

Noise numbs. Silence awakens.

F. Worship Throughout the Day

Worship turns awareness into intimacy.

9. PRESENCE CREATES OVERFLOW

Overflow is not the product of effort; it is the product of abiding. The more you sit with Jesus, the more your life will look like Jesus. The more time you spend with Him, the more His presence pours from you. Presence turns you into a fountain.

REFLECTION

1. How do you most naturally experience the presence of God?

2. What practices help you abide rather than rush through spiritual moments?

3. Where do you need to slow down and make space for intimacy with God?

4. What emotions arise when you think about stillness before God?

5. How might daily awareness of His presence transform your attitude and actions?

CHAPTER 10

Pouring in Community and Healthy Relationships

Overflow was never meant to be a solo experience. God pours into you *personally*, but He sustains you *relationally*. From the beginning, God declared: **"It is not good for man to be alone"** (Genesis 2:18). This wasn't a romantic statement. It was a theological one. Human beings are not designed to flourish in isolation. We are shaped vessels to pour into; and be poured into by others.

A solitary Christian eventually becomes a **leaking** Christian. A connected Christian becomes an **overflowing** Christian.

1. GOD USES PEOPLE TO STRENGTHEN YOUR CONTAINER

Every major move of God in Scripture involved people:

- Moses needed Aaron and Hur
- David needed Jonathan
- Elijah needed Elisha

- Naomi needed Ruth
- Paul needed Barnabas, Silas, Timothy
- Jesus Himself surrounded Himself with the Twelve

The Kingdom of God does not grow through lone heroes—it grows through **godly community**.

Proverbs says: **"As iron sharpens iron, so one person sharpens another"** (Proverbs 27:17).

Community shapes you.
Community strengthens you.
Community protects you.
Community enlarges your capacity.

2. THE DANGER OF ISOLATION

The enemy loves isolation because isolation weakens the vessel even when the believer is sincere. Solomon warns: **"Whoever isolates himself seeks his own desire; he breaks out against all sound judgment"** (Proverbs 18:1, ESV). Isolation leads to:

- distorted thinking
- emotional instability
- spiritual dryness
- exaggerated fears
- weakened resistance to temptation
- self-deception
- loneliness
- unhealed wounds

Isolation is one of the enemy's oldest strategies. If he can get you alone, he can get you vulnerable. Even lions hunt by isolating their prey. Peter uses the same imagery: **"Your enemy the devil**

prowls around like a roaring lion" (1 Peter 5:8). The safe sheep is not the strongest; it is the closest to the flock.

3. COMMUNITY IS GOD'S METHOD OF OVERFLOW

The early Church was a community overflowing with love, generosity, prayer, and power: **"They shared everything ... there were no needy persons among them ... and the Lord added to their number daily"** (Acts 2:44–47).

Why was the early Church unstoppable? Because they were together. Where unity flows, the Spirit flows. Psalm 133 says: **"Where brothers dwell together in unity, *there the Lord commands the blessing*"** (Psalm 133:1–3, emphasis added). Unity is the environment of overflow.

Dorcas (Tabitha) – Acts 9: She served the poor. When she died, the community wept. A life poured out leaves a legacy.

4. HEALTHY RELATIONSHIPS FILL—UNHEALTHY RELATIONSHIPS DRAIN

You are a vessel, and relationships are either:

- funnels that fill you
- or cracks that drain you

A single unhealthy relationship can drain:

- confidence
- peace
- identity
- energy
- emotional strength
- spiritual focus

Scripture says: **"Bad company corrupts good character"** (1 Corinthians 15:33).

God isn't calling you to be suspicious; but He *is* calling you to be discerning.

5. THE THREE KINDS OF RELATIONSHIPS EVERY BELIEVER NEEDS

A. A Paul: Someone Who Pours into You

A mentor.
A spiritual covering.
A guide.

B. A Barnabas: Someone Who Walks with You

A peer.
A friend.
A companion.

C. A Timothy: Someone You Pour Into

A disciple.
A younger believer.
A spiritual son or daughter.

Overflow is sustained when you are being poured into *and* actively pouring into others. It is the rhythm of heaven:

Receive → Overflow → Pour → Receive Again

6. THE ILLUSTRATION: THE THREE-POURED CUP

In Middle Eastern hospitality, the host pours three cups:

- the **first cup** is ordinary
- the **second cup** is generous
- the **third cup** is overflowing; the "cup of friendship"

Overflow is a relational gift; not something you drink alone.

7. HOW TO BUILD GODLY COMMUNITY

A. Pursue Depth, Not Just Proximity

Sitting in church rows is not the same as spiritual connection.

B. Be Vulnerable

Healing flows where honesty flows.

C. Choose Friends Who Strengthen Your Soul

Walk with people who make you love God more.

D. Set Boundaries

Protect your peace.

E. Serve Together

Community grows strongest in shared mission.

8. GOD WANTS TO FILL YOUR LIFE WITH PEOPLE WHO BUILD, NOT BREAK

You were never called to walk alone. You were called to walk together. Overflow grows in the soil of community.

REFLECTION

1. Who has been a significant source of spiritual strength in your life?

2. Which relationships drain you, and which relationships fill you?

3. Where do you need stronger boundaries to protect your spiritual health?

4. What type of community do you need in this season—mentor, friend, accountability, fellowship?

5. How can you intentionally pour into someone else this week?

CHAPTER 11

Pouring in Purpose, Serving, and Sacrifice

Overflow is not only about what God pours **into** you. It is about what God pours **through** you. You are not a reservoir. You are a river. A life that overflows is a life aligned with divine purpose; a life willing to serve, give, love, and sacrifice.

Purpose expands capacity.
Serving sharpens character.
Sacrifice deepens joy.

1. PURPOSE WAS GIVEN BEFORE WORK EXISTED

Before the fall, before sin, before struggle, Genesis says: **"The Lord God placed the man in the Garden to work it and take care of it"** (Genesis 2:15).

Work was not punishment.
Purpose was not a curse.
Purpose is part of the divine design of humanity.

You were created to *contribute*—not just exist.

2. PURPOSE IS NOT SOMETHING YOU FIND—IT IS SOMETHING YOU ALIGN WITH

Many believers scramble to "discover their purpose," but purpose is not something you stumble into. Purpose flows from:

- identity
- intimacy
- obedience
- calling
- gifting
- passion
- Spirit-filled desire

In Scripture, God never said: "Go find your purpose." He said: "Follow Me." Purpose unfolds in the footsteps of obedience.

3. PURPOSE EXPANDS THE VESSEL

When you are living with purpose:

- your energy increases
- your joy deepens
- your clarity sharpens
- your capacity grows
- your vessel enlarges

Doing what God created you to do increases your spiritual volume. Jeremiah said: **"His word is in my heart like a fire … I am weary of holding it in"** (Jeremiah 20:9).

Purpose is fire. Fire expands.

4. SERVING IS THE PATHWAY TO GREATNESS

Jesus overturned the world's hierarchy when He said: **"The greatest among you will be your servant"** (Matthew 23:11).

In the Kingdom of God:

- greatness comes through humility
- promotion comes through service
- honor comes through sacrifice
- overflow comes through pouring out

You are never more like Jesus than when you serve. For Jesus said: **"The Son of Man did not come to be served, but to serve, and give His life"** (Mark 10:45).

5. SACRIFICE MAKES ROOM FOR GOD'S POWER

Every breakthrough in Scripture required sacrifice:

- Abraham laid Isaac on the altar
- Moses laid down privilege
- Ruth laid down her home
- David laid down reputation
- Esther risked her life
- Jesus laid down everything

Sacrifice is not losing—it is sowing. And God never ignores sacrifice. David said: **"I will not offer to the Lord that which costs me nothing"** (2 Samuel 24:24).

Sacrifice enlarges your vessel so God can pour more into you.

6. THE ILLUSTRATION: THE OLIVE PRESS

Olive oil: a symbol of anointing comes from pressure. The olive must be crushed. The oil flows from sacrifice.

Likewise, the greatest anointing on a believer's life often flows from seasons of surrender and sacrifice.

7. YOUR LIFE WILL ALWAYS OVERFLOW MOST WHERE YOU SERVE MOST

Your gifts are not for you. Your calling is not for you. Your anointing is not for you.

They are for:

- the Church
- the world
- the broken
- the hungry
- the lost
- the next generation

Purpose is outward. Overflow is outward. God pours so you can pour.

REFLECTION

1. What do you sense God calling you to in this season?

2. How does serving others affect your joy and spiritual vitality?

3. Where have you experienced God filling you as you pour out?

4. What gifts, passions, or experiences may be part of your purpose?

5. What step of obedience or sacrifice is God inviting you to take?

CHAPTER 12

Overflowing Joy That Touches the World

Your overflow is not the end of the story; it is the beginning of someone else's. Overflow is not a personal spiritual experience; it is a **missional assignment**. God wants to turn your life into a river that brings joy, hope, healing, and transformation wherever you go. Jesus said: **"Whoever believes in Me ... rivers of living water will flow from within them"** (John 7:38).

Not a lake.
Not a puddle.
Not a cup.

Rivers.

Rivers flow outward.
Rivers shape landscapes.
Rivers give life.
Rivers bring refreshing.
Rivers carve paths.
Rivers change everything they touch.

1. OVERFLOW IS GOD'S STRATEGY FOR THE WORLD

God spreads His Kingdom through overflowing vessels:

- Joseph's overflow saved nations
- Daniel's overflow influenced kings
- Esther's overflow preserved her people
- Paul's overflow birthed churches
- The early Church's overflow turned the world upside down

The Gospel is carried through people overflowing with Jesus.

2. YOUR OVERFLOW IS SOMEONE ELSE'S ANSWERED PRAYER

- Someone is praying for the encouragement you will bring.
- Someone is praying for the smile you will give.
- Someone is praying for a word you will speak.
- Someone is praying for hope that will flow from your story.
- Someone is praying for comfort that will flow from your healing.

You are part of God's response to the cries of the world.

3. OVERFLOWING JOY IS EVANGELISM WITHOUT STRIVING

You don't have to force evangelism. Joy is magnetic. Nehemiah said: **"The joy of the Lord is your strength"** (Nehemiah 8:10).

Joy is not only strength—joy is fragrance. A joyful believer is a walking testimony.

4. OVERFLOW TURNS YOUR PAIN INTO MINISTRY

Your past becomes someone else's hope.
Your healing becomes someone else's map.
Your restoration becomes someone else's courage.

Second Corinthians 1:4 says: **"He comforts us ... so that we can comfort others."**

Overflow is divine recycling. God takes what the enemy meant for harm and pours it out as healing for others.

5. OVERFLOW MAKES YOU DANGEROUS TO DARKNESS

A believer overflowing with joy is:

- untouchable in spirit
- unshakable in faith
- unstoppable in purpose

Hell fears an overflowing believer. Because overflowing believers:

- love deeply
- forgive quickly
- serve joyfully
- pray persistently
- shine brightly
- worship boldly
- endure faithfully

Overflow carries spiritual authority.

6. ILLUSTRATION: THE RIVER THAT CARVES STONE

Rivers over time carve through rock. Not because they push harder, but because they flow consistently. Your daily overflow: your love, your joy, your presence, will carve through the hardest hearts and the darkest places. Not through force but through flow.

7. OVERFLOW IS LEGACY

Overflow is not what you accomplish, it is who you become.
It is the river of your life that continues after you.

What spills from your life:

- into your children
- into your grandchildren
- into your community
- into your church
- into your generation

That is your legacy. You were made to overflow beyond your years.

8. THE INVITATION

Do you want to live a life that touches the world?

Then allow God to:

- heal your container
- strengthen your vessel
- fill you daily
- keep you connected
- pour you out generously

Overflow is not your responsibility. Overflow is your inheritance. Just stay under the flow and God will handle the overflow.

REFLECTION

1. Where is God inviting you to bring your overflow right now?

2. Who in your life needs the joy, hope, or peace that overflows from you?

3. What would it look like to embody the presence of Jesus in your daily environments?

4. What legacy of overflow do you want to build?

5. How will you stay connected to the Source so you can keep filling, pouring, and overflowing?

CONCLUSION

The Commission to Live the Overflow Life

You have journeyed through twelve chapters with a journey of healing and strengthening, of truth and transformation, of uncovering cracks and discovering capacity. But more than anything else, this has been a journey back to the heart of Jesus. Because the Overflow Life is not about a book. Not about a metaphor. Not about techniques or disciplines. Not even about personal spiritual progress. It is about **Him**. It is about union with Christ, life in Christ, joy from Christ, and overflow through Christ. Jesus said: **"I have told you these things so that you will be filled with My joy. Yes, your joy will overflow!"** (John 15:11, NLT).

This is not a suggestion. This is not an exaggeration. This is not a poetic phrase. This is a **promise**.

A promise from the One who does not lie.
A promise from the One who finished what He started.
A promise from the One who is the same yesterday, today, and forever.

Overflow is not a fantasy.
Overflow is not for the spiritually elite.
Overflow is not for a select few.

Overflow is the normal Christian life.

You were made for this.

1. YOU ARE A VESSEL FORMED BY THE POTTER

You may have cracks—He heals them.
You may feel fragile—He strengthens you.
You may feel inadequate—He fills you.
You may feel unknown—He calls you.
You may feel unworthy—He covers you.

The Potter does not discard clay that collapses. He refashions it.

You are not your past.
You are not your wounds.
You are not your failures.
You are not your fears.
You are not your weakness.

You are His workmanship.
His vessel.
His creation.
His instrument.
His beloved.

And He is not done forming you.

2. YOUR CRACKS WERE NEVER A DISQUALIFICATION—THEY WERE AN INVITATION

The enemy says:

"You're too broken."
"You're too wounded."
"You're too inconsistent."
"You're too sinful."
"You're too scarred."

But God says:

"My grace is sufficient" (2 Corinthians 12:9).
"I am making all things new" (Revelation 21:5).
"I will restore you" (Joel 2:25).
"I will strengthen you" (1 Peter 5:10).
"You are Mine" (Isaiah 43:1).

What disqualified you in the world qualifies you in the Kingdom.

Your healed places will become holy places.
Your restored places will become radiant places.
Your scars will become testimonies.

Where you once leaked, you will now overflow.

3. THE FATHER DELIGHTS TO FILL YOU

He is not reluctant.
He is not withholding.
He is not stingy.

The Father fills eagerly, generously, joyfully. Jesus said: **"How much more will your Father give the Holy Spirit to those who ask?"** (Luke 11:13).

The Father is more ready to fill you than you are ready to be filled. He fills through:

- His Word
- His Presence
- His Spirit
- His people
- His purpose
- His love

There is no limit to His pouring except the size of your container.

Enlarge it.
Lift it.
Offer it.
He will fill it.

4. OVERFLOW IS NOT THE END OF THE JOURNEY—IT IS THE BEGINNING

God does not fill you for you alone. He fills you for:

- your family
- your church
- your community
- your workplace
- the broken
- the weary
- the lost
- the overlooked

Overflow is the divine strategy for touching the world.

Your life becomes:

- a light in darkness
- a river in dry places
- a shelter in storms
- a witness to the Gospel
- a carrier of God's presence
- a vessel of healing
- a fountain of joy

Your overflow becomes someone else's encounter with Jesus.

5. YOU ARE SENT OUT WITH JOY

Isaiah prophesied: **"You will go out with joy and be led forth with peace"** (Isaiah 55:12).

This is your commission. Go out with:

- renewed joy
- strengthened faith
- restored identity
- healed wounds
- enlarged capacity
- purified motives
- revived passion
- restored peace

The world does not need more Christians trying harder. The world needs more Christians overflowing. You are that believer.

You are the vessel God will use.
You are the river He will release.
You are the light He will shine.
You are the ambassador He will send.

6. YOUR LIFE WILL BECOME A TESTIMONY OF WHAT GOD CAN DO THROUGH AN AVAILABLE VESSEL

The journey is not over—it has transformed.

You will walk differently.

Pray differently.
Love differently.
Serve differently.
Worship differently.
Lead differently.
Live differently.

Not because you are striving—but because you are filled.

Not because you are perfect—but because you are healed.

Not because you are strong—but because His strength flows through you.

7. A BLESSING FOR THE JOURNEY AHEAD

May your heart remain soft before the Potter.
May your cracks become gold-filled places of glory.
May your vessel be strengthened daily.
May your soul be anchored in Scripture.
May your life be saturated with presence.
May your habits build holy rhythms.
May your relationships be sources of life.
May your purpose set your heart ablaze.
May your joy rise above circumstances.
May your overflow bless generations.
May your entire life become a river flowing from the throne of God.

May you never settle for emptiness when you were created to overflow.

This is your calling.
This is your inheritance.
This is your life.

The Overflow Life.

THE AQUEDUCT

Ancient Roman aqueducts carried water from mountains to cities.

They were not reservoirs.
They were **channels**.

The water that changed cities never stayed in the aqueduct—it flowed through it.

That is the overflow life.

From Empty to Overflowing

WEEK 1: REPAIR THE VESSEL

Healing the Leaks That Drain Your Life

Day 1 – Awareness: You Are the Vessel

Scripture: 2 Corinthians 4:7

Practice: Sit quietly for 5 minutes and ask: "Lord, what is the condition of my vessel?"

Reflection: Where do I feel most empty right now?

Day 2 – Identifying the Leaks

Scripture: Psalm 139:23–24

Practice: Journal honestly: Where is my life leaking joy (wounds, sin, habits, stress)?

Reflection: What drains me the most consistently?

Day 3 – Unhealed Wounds

Scripture: Psalm 147:3

Practice: Name one past wound you've avoided. Bring it to God in prayer.

Reflection: How has this wound affected my joy?

Day 4 – Truth Over Lies

Scripture: John 8:32

Practice: Identify one lie you believe (e.g., "I'm not enough"). Replace it with Scripture.

Reflection: What truth do I need to anchor in today?

Day 5 – Confession and Cleansing

Scripture: 1 John 1:9

Practice: Confess any known sin honestly to God.

Reflection: How do I feel after bringing this into the light?

Day 6 – Breaking Emotional Clutter

Scripture: Psalm 46:10

Practice: 10 minutes of silence—no phone, no noise. Just be with God.

Reflection: What emotions surfaced when I slowed down?

Day 7 – Surrender

Scripture: Matthew 11:28–30

Practice: Write down burdens you're carrying. Pray and release them to God.

Reflection: What am I holding that God never asked me to carry?

WEEK 2: FILL THE VESSEL

Establishing Rhythms That Sustain Fullness

Day 8 – The Word as Foundation

Scripture: Matthew 4:4

Practice: Read a chapter of Scripture slowly (suggest: John 15).

Reflection: What word or phrase stands out to me?

Day 9 – Meditating on Scripture

Scripture: Psalm 1:2–3

Practice: Repeat one verse throughout the day.

Reflection: How did staying in the Word affect my thoughts?

Day 10 – The Presence of God

Scripture: Psalm 16:11

Practice: Spend 10–15 minutes in worship (music or quiet adoration).

Reflection: What changed in me during His presence?

Day 11 – Practicing Abiding

Scripture: John 15:4–5

Practice: Throughout the day, pause and whisper: "I remain in You."

Reflection: When did I feel most connected to God today?

Day 12 – Prayer as Connection

Scripture: Philippians 4:6–7

Practice: Turn every worry today into a prayer.

Reflection: Did prayer reduce my anxiety?

Day 13 – Building Healthy Habits

Scripture: Hebrews 2:1

Practice: Choose one daily habit to begin (Scripture, prayer, gratitude).

Reflection: What habit will strengthen my vessel long-term?

Day 14 – Community Matters

Scripture: Proverbs 27:17

Practice: Reach out to a trusted believer for encouragement or prayer.

Reflection: How do relationships affect my spiritual health?

WEEK 3: LIVE THE OVERFLOW

Letting What God Fills Flow Outward

Day 15 – You Are a River

Scripture: John 7:38

Practice: Ask: "Lord, who can I bless today?" Then act on it.

Reflection: Who was impacted by what flowed from me?

Day 16 – Serving Others

Scripture: Mark 10:45

Practice: Do one intentional act of service (small or hidden).

Reflection: How did serving affect my joy?

Day 17 – Encouragement as Overflow

Scripture: 1 Thessalonians 5:11

Practice: Speak or send encouragement to three people.

Reflection: How did giving encouragement affect my spirit?

Day 18 – Generosity

Scripture: Acts 20:35

Practice: Give something—time, money, attention, kindness.

Reflection: What did generosity reveal about my heart?

Day 19 – Sharing Your Story

Scripture: 2 Corinthians 1:4

Practice: Share a testimony or personal story with someone.

Reflection: How can my healing help others?

Day 20 – Living with Purpose

Scripture: Ephesians 2:10

Practice: Ask God: "Where are You sending me?" Write what you sense.

Reflection: Where do I feel most alive and aligned with purpose?

Day 21 – A Life of Overflow

Scripture: Romans 15:13

Practice: Reflect on the past 21 days. Write what God has done in you.

Reflection: What does "overflow" now mean in my life?

Final Declaration

I am a vessel God is healing.
I am a vessel God is filling.
I am a vessel God is using.

I will not live empty.
I will not live drained.
I will live in the overflow of Christ.

Afterword

In John 10:10 Jesus said, "I am come that they might have life, and that they might have it more abundantly." Every born-again child of God has life. Romans 6:23 says, "the gift of God is eternal life through Jesus Christ our Lord." So every Christian has life. But the Bible says it is possible for a Christian not only to have life, but to have a life that is a full and overflowing life.

He begins in Romans 1:16 by giving us the theme of his letter, "For I am not ashamed of the gospel of Christ: for it is the power of God unto salvation to everyone who believes." In Romans 15:8–13, Paul brings us to the climax he has been discussing in the book of Romans.

He starts in Romans by **explaining** to us that we were **polluted in sin**. Next, he **encourages** us that we were **pardoned through the Son**. Last, he **expands** us through the **power of the Spirit**. We not only have life, but we have the abundant life! In Romans 15:13, we read, "Now the God of hope fill you with all joy and peace in believing, that you may abound (overflow) in hope, through the power of the Holy Spirit."

God never intended for people who come to know Christ as their Savior to just merely get by. God wants you to have life like a full and overflowing fountain. God wants your life to be like rivers of water. There is nothing worse than a half-filled Christian trying to overflow.

THE SOURCE OF THE OVERFLOW LIFE

When you come to Christ as your Savior, the Bible teaches that the Holy Spirit comes to dwell in your heart. God Himself, in the person of the Holy Spirit, comes to dwell in your heart. The Holy Spirit makes real in us what Jesus did for us at the cross of Calvary.

He begins in verse 13: "Now the God of hope fill you ...". Isn't that a marvelous title for God? Isn't it wonderful to know that we have a great God in heaven, our Father, who encourages our heart? Do you ever get down in the dumps? I have good news for you. You can come to the God who is the God of consolation and He will encourage your heart.

Paul tells us in verse 13 that God is the God of hope. This world is desperately looking for hope. This world is desperately looking for a life that has some meaning and a life that has a future to it. Here is the source of the full and overflowing life. God has a monopoly on it.

There are some things you can only get from God. You can only get comfort, ultimately, from God. You can't go down to the neighborhood store and ask for three yards of hope. You can't go to the hardware store and ask for two-gallon buckets of hope. God is the God of hope. If you want hope, you have to come to God. There is no hope apart from God.

There is no abundant, overflowing life apart from the God of hope, who can fill you to overflowing. God is an expert on life. If you want to know about life, you have to come to God. It is God who gave us life; it is God who gives us eternal life, and if we want the full and abundant life, we must come to God to get it. The God of hope wants to fill us.

THE SCOPE OF THE OVERFLOW LIFE

Not only the **source** of this overflowing life, but look at the **scope** of it. Notice the three words, "joy, peace, hope." He says, "the God of hope fill you to overflowing with all joy and peace and hope." Joy, peace, and hope are things people are looking for today. They are spending a fortune and traveling all over the world, trying everything there is to try. Yet, the Bible says if you want joy and peace and hope, you can get all three of them from the Lord.

The first word is "joy." Everybody wants to be happy. I don't know of anybody who says, "My goal in life is to be as miserable as I possibly can." I don't know of anybody who says, "I hope I live the life of misery, never have any joy, never have any happiness."

The Bible says you have all joy from the God of hope, in believing in the power of the Holy Spirit. He is saying if you want to be happy, you can get happiness from the Lord. Happiness is not found in pleasures. A lot of people think if you just have enough pleasure you'll be happy. The Bible talks about the pleasures of sin for a season. Then, there's that bitter aftertaste of sin.

Other people think, *I'll find joy in pleasant circumstances. If I can just get my circumstances right, get a comfortable home, get a good car, get money in the bank, get my circumstances pleasant.* Yet when you study the Bible, you will find out that these early Christians were filled to overflowing with joy, and yet they were experiencing persecution, uncertainties concerning their own personal affairs. But in the midst of it all, they experienced an abundant, overflowing joy.

In John 15:11, Jesus said, "These things have I spoken unto you, that my joy might remain in you, and that your joy might be full." Jesus talked about His joy the night before the cross.

Just ahead was the kiss of the traitor and hiss of the whip and the bloody path of the cross, and yet Jesus was talking about His joy. I'm talking about having a hallelujah chorus in your heart regardless of what's going on outside of your life.

That second word is "peace." People want peace, don't they? People are looking anywhere and everywhere trying to find peace. I'm talking about that inner tranquility, that calmness of spirit. I'm talking about that depth of the soul that gives people a sense of inner calm.

It says the God of all hope can fill you to overflowing with His peace. We do not get peace in pills. We get peace in a person, the Lord Jesus Christ. In John 14:27, Jesus said again the night before His crucifixion, "Peace I leave with you, my peace I give unto you: not as the world gives, give I unto you. Let not your heart be troubled, neither let it be afraid." What would people give for peace today? If we want peace, we get peace from the God of peace. That's the full and overflowing life.

The third word is "hope." The word doesn't just mean wishing something will come out good. There's more to the word "hope" than just a strong wish. Hope means a confidence in the future. God can fill your life full and to overflowing with confidence about the future. If you know Jesus Christ as your personal Savior, today your future is filled with hope. But if you are not a Christian, if you do not know Christ as your personal Savior, whatever the future holds for you is not good but bad. I have news for you if you know Christ as Savior. Everything is going to turn out good. He's going to fill you to overflowing with hope for the future. You have it made in the future.

In 1 Corinthians 3:21, we read, "All things are yours." Everything is yours, that is if you are saved. "Whether Paul or Apollos or Cephas (that is the preachers, they are all yours). The world is yours. Your sky is looking real good today. This world is yours. You see all the beautiful trees. Your trees are growing well today. This world is yours. "Life is yours." "Death is yours." Death for a child of God is not a thing in the world but a shuttle bus that carries you from this world to a better world.

THE SECRET OF THE OVERFLOWING LIFE

The source of the full and overflowing life is the God of hope. The scope of it is joy and peace and hope. The **secret** of it is "in believing in the power of the Holy Spirit." God the Father **promises** this abundant life. God the Son, the Lord Jesus, **purchased** this abundant life. But God the Holy Spirit in your heart **provides** this abundant life. The Holy Spirit can make possible everything necessary for your life to be full and overflowing.

Yet Paul says the secret is "in believing." He is saying that it is by faith that we appropriate everything God has made available for us in the person of the Holy Spirit to live the full and overflowing life.

You may say, "I just can't believe. I just don't have enough faith." Yes, you can believe. You can believe that God can give you this joy and this peace and hope. You already have faith. Romans 12:3 says, "God has dealt to every person a measure of faith." We live by faith every day. Every day of your life you have enough to get through one day.

Have you ever thought what it would be to try to live one day without faith? Think about it. Let's imagine one day without faith. You wake up that morning in a fever of fear. It's time to get up, but you are afraid to put your feet on the floor because you are afraid the boards are rotten and you may go straight in. So you cautiously get up and go to the bathroom to brush your teeth, but you are afraid to brush your teeth. You're afraid the water is polluted.

Now it is time to eat breakfast because you are hungry, but you will not eat because you are afraid the food is contaminated. You are living a day without faith.

You go out to the car and get in to go to work, but you will not get in the car. The worker who assembled that car may not have put the steering wheel in correctly and you may get in a wreck. You are living a day without faith.

So you have to walk all the way downtown to work. About midmorning you come into work. You walk in the building. It's a day without faith. You walk over to the elevator and can't get on it because the elevator may not work. Thus, you climb the stairs to the tenth floor to your office.

Upon your arrival to the office, you are suspicious of everybody. You are living a day without faith. Lunch time comes. How would you like to share a ham sandwich? No, afraid to eat it—might have poison in it.

You walk home and your spouse has a marvelous meal prepared and laid out on the table. Yet, you will not eat it because you are suspicious of your spouse. Last but not least, you are not sure if these children are really yours. You go to bed totally exhausted because you have lived a day without faith!

We live every day by a measure of faith. The secret to the abundant, overflowing life is "in believing." We have the source, the scope, and the secret. I encourage you to step out into the world

God has for you and believe that the power of the Spirit will give you the victorious Christian life!

—**Dr. James O. Davis,** President & Founder,
Global Church Network

About the Author

Rev. Ejaz Nabie is the Lead Pastor of Faith Assembly Church in Richmond Hill, New York. Called by grace out of a Muslim background, his life is a living testimony to the transforming power of the Gospel. With a heart for the nations and a passion for spiritual formation, he has become a trusted voice to believers seeking to live with wisdom, purpose, and faithfulness.

Beyond his pastoral work, Pastor Ejaz serves as the Executive Producer for Global Events with the Global Church Network, helping to unite and equip leaders across the world for the advancement of God's Kingdom.

A gifted communicator and visionary leader, he has ministered at conferences and churches around the globe. His unique blend of spiritual depth, cultural awareness, and practical insight invites readers and listeners alike to pursue a life shaped by God's truth and empowered by His Spirit.

Through his writing, Pastor Ejaz calls believers to embrace the discipline that leads to divine success—a life rooted in wisdom, shaped by grace, and lived for the glory of God.

www.ingramcontent.com/pod-product-compliance
Lightning Source LLC
LaVergne TN
LVHW090612110826
845146LV00001B/361